Eye of the Island
Olho da Ilha

"This collaborative translation of Corsino Fortes's impassioned and oracular poetry is an important and rich resource for the English-language reader. Fortes's poems inhabit an earth made flesh, and although the poems concern Cape Verde and its bloody colonial history, they reach always for the universal in suffering and oppression."
– Sasha Dugdale

"Geology and geography collide in Corsino Fortes's poetry to create a complex genealogy of feelings towards memory and colonialism, and the African landscape and mind-scape. With volcanic candour, these eloquently translated poems speak of 'Sun and carbon joining / The body and soul' and capture the solitude and solidarity of everyday life where realism and metaphysics are quotidian like our sun and bread."
– Kit Fan

"I would recommend this magnificent, generous, and bilingual presentation of Corsino Fortes's work to anyone who enjoys grappling with the poignant, the sensuous, and the esoteric."
– Asymptote Journal

Corsino Fortes

Eye of the Island
Olho da Ilha

Translated from Portuguese by
Daniel Hahn with Sean O'Brien

First published in 2025
by the Poetry Translation Centre Ltd
The Albany, Douglas Way, London, SE8 4AG

www.poetrytranslation.org

Poems © Corsino Fortes and Dom Quixote Publishers, 2001
English Translations © Daniel Hahn and Sean O'Brien 2015
Introduction © Daniel Hahn 2025
Afterword © Romalyn Ante 2025

Print ISBN: 978-1-7384701-4-3
E-ISBN: 978-1-7384701-6-7

These translations first appeared as part of *Selected Poems*
(Archipelago Books, New York, 2015)

A catalogue record for this book is available from the British Library

Typeset in Minion by Poetry Translation Centre Ltd

Series Editor: Nashwa Nasreldin
Cover Design: Kit Humphrey
Printed in the UK by T.J. Books

The PTC is supported using public funding by
Arts Council England

Contents

Introduction	6
Proposition	12
Message to Umbertona	14
Earth to Earth	18
Gate of the Sun	20
There is a Dead Ship at the Citadel	24
When Morning Breaks	26
Island	30
Root and Face	32
Today I Want Only to be a Drum in the Heart of the Baobab	38
Pollen for Your Mouth	44
Mestizo : Mestiza	48
Oracle	50
The Caesarean of Three Continents	52
I Pass Through the Days	56
Sunflower	58
Afterword	60
About the contributors	64
About the series	66

Introduction

Born and brought up on the Cape Verdean island of São Vicente, Corsino Fortes studied in Portugal and spent much of his working life abroad, so while his work is concerned with giving voice to the life of his own country, its violent colonial past and possible futures, his perspective is often that of an exile, and he has haunting exile and redemptive return among his recurring themes. He writes in Cape Verdean Creole, as well as Portuguese (usually one translated into the other, occasionally blending the two together) – a choice that in itself says much about the country's identity. Fortes began writing in the dying days of colonial rule, and he uses his work to reclaim, almost to recreate, his newly reborn country. But these are not the sort of political poems that deal with the country's governments, leaders or freedom-fighting heroes; rather they present the living islands almost mythically – a place imbued with creative, regenerative forces.

The poems in this collection have mostly been taken from the first three of Fortes's four published collections and come from an expanded selection published by Archipelago Books in 2015; some were originally translated for a PTC commission back in 2007. While Fortes wrote in two languages, with his blessing, our translations were mostly based on his Portuguese versions and did not distinguish between the two (I would have thought differently about this today); both languages are represented among the source poems in this volume.

I began by producing functional versions, which sought (impossibly, of course) to render each poem clearly and cleanly into English while resisting any impulse to tidy, to polish, to make any aesthetic or interpretative choices at all. My aim was not to narrow down to particular decisions, but to open up the multiple possibilities a poem could encompass. The lines were often annotated with divergent options, glosses on the source or useful background information. ("That 'rotcha scribida' means 'written rock', but NB also refers to one specific famous rock in CV with inscriptions as yet undeciphered. There's a Cesária Évora song, too.")

Here, for example, is my 'literal' of 'Há navio morto na cidadela':

There is (a) dead ship [=common word] in/at the citadel [citadela]

There are dead ships in/at the old city [cidade velha]

A/One child crosses the island between/amid
drums The shrub/bush gives a hand full/filled with earth
And places the seeds close to the [ten-string] guitars [sthg called a *viola*]

Two children go/skirt around the mouth of the riverbank
    [I think? – checking…]
With a rooster's song [±cockcrow] in the vena cava
                    And they awake/wake
With their knuckles [in Pt it's always 'the knuckles of their fingers']
The prow/bow of the/their faces
Of/From dead oars in the west

Three children go round

> the steps of the district/county And
> Tear/Grab/Snatch [arrancam] from the flesh
> The anchors [âncoras] of finding
> The ships [more literary word – eg. barques] of (the) Discovery

These versions – useful, if ugly – were then handed over to Sean O'Brien. From that point on, my job would be to cast an eye over Sean's work with the source in mind, and draw attention to misunderstandings, or moments where I felt the English poem had strayed too far from its Portuguese-language moorings. This is not, incidentally, a common experience for a translator; usually, we find ourselves straining slightly against the source, pulling away to see if we can get a bit more slack, but in this process I was (and I don't mean to sound antagonistic) 'on the same side' as the source, pulling against the new version – the role usually reserved for the naturally protective translated writer, whose representative I had to be.

The voice in Fortes's work is not one that renders easily in English. It's often declamatory and dramatically musical, which can come off as, at best, a little arch and archaic, at worst portentous and hollow.

In addition, the poems use recurring imagery that likely resonated with a Cape Verdean reader, but which more often than not have no near-mythical associations for an Anglophone one. (The recurrent motifs have implications for vocabulary, too, which suited me as their first-stage translator – I didn't know the Portuguese words for mortar and pestle when I started the process, but having looked them up I then got to recycle them, using them again and again, in poem after poem after poem…) Many of these recurring images and words, small-scale and large – a symbology comprising pestle, guitar, sun, beach, bread… – are physical, inanimate things assigned vital and sometimes epic creative power.

The poems are strong and sonorous, inhabited by these recurring images and other potent visual moments, and unpicking each of these into its components – yes, such-and-such a word means this, but there are elements of that in it, too, and echoes of the other – was a pleasing challenge. My readings of the poems always sought to allow Sean possibilities, not close them off – they were non-committal, expansive. The harder part of the job would come next, and that would be all down to Sean.

Fortes's poems, as Sean has written, move between "vivid observation and impassioned declamation". The translator's challenge, then, was "to accommodate the elevated, exclamatory character of the poems without sounding empty and inflated, as surrealism (a clear reference point) often does in English. Against this, Fortes marshals an extraordinarily subtle, sustained and powerful rhythmic life, able to speak to the auditory imagination of the non-Lusophone. The impression is of magnificently controlled lyric improvisation."

The original PTC commission was the first time I'd agreed to translate poetry, having always doubted my own ability to make poetic lines work. I retain that doubt today, but if I understand that skill any better now, it's from examining Sean's versions of my translations of the Fortes work.

Here's that same poem again:

There Is a Dead Ship at the Citadel

There are dead ships at the old city

A child crosses the island to the sound of drums
A bush offers a handful of earth

And spreads the seeds near the ten-string guitars

Two children skirt the river-mouth
At cock-crow in the vena cava
                        With their knuckles
They awaken
The prows of their faces
From dreams of dead oars in the west

The children wander
            the stairways of the neighbourhood
And draw from the flesh
            The anchors of discovery
            The caravels of exploration

Often the thing that struck me when I read Sean's renderings of Fortes's poems, was how little he had actually changed; what struck me next, however, was how much difference those little changes had made. Opting for this word rather than that (not ship or barque, but caravel), changing the weighting of a phrase, moving the spring in the line by a syllable one way or another – and suddenly it sounded precise, deliberate, in focus. Juxtaposed lines didn't always follow a clear thread of sense, but in such cases, what Sean privileged in Fortes's work was what he described as "the authenticity of the rhythmic impulse". To someone like me who had never understood how this happens, the transformation was sort of magical – no, that's not the right word, because it wasn't mysterious exactly, it was sort of the opposite, in fact: it was an insight into the mechanics – watching a conjuror in slow motion, one frame at a time, to see how the apparently magical effect is actually achieved.

Daniel Hahn

Poems

Proposição

Ano a ano
      crânio a crânio
Rostos contornam
      o olho da ilha
Com poços de pedra
      abertos
          no olho da cabra

E membros de terra
            Explodem
Na boca das ruas
      Estátuas de pão só
      Estátuas de pão sol

Ano a ano
      crânio a crânio
Tambores rompem
      a promessa da terra
Com pedras
Devolvendo às bocas
As suas veias
      De muitos remos

Proposition

Year by year
       skull by skull
Faces circle
       the eye of the island
Where stone wells
       open
       in a goat's eye

And the earth's limbs
           Erupt
In the mouths of the streets
       Statue of bread alone
       Statue of the sun's bread

Year by year
       skull by skull
Drums break
       the promise of the earth
With rocks
Restoring to the mouths
The lode
       Of many oars

Recode d'Umbertona

Umbertona! manhã
             'ma ta ba lançode pa s'ilha
Bô ca tem n'hum sinal d'amor
        pame levâ bos gente?

Não 'm ta sec
        broken
        dsorientode c'ma carangueje

Ma bô ca tem
    n'nhum cantiga d'exilode
Daquês sem palmanha
    nem boquinha de note
    pame levâ boca de pove?

Bai! bô dzê Soncente
c'ma sombre dnha corpe ê cruz
Longe de sol dnha terra
        ta rolâ na África
        ta rolâ n'Iropa
        ta rolâ na Merca
        ta rolâ na mapa
        ta rolâ na munde

Bai! bô dzê Porte-Grande
Pa ca tchomo-me sodade

Paquê nha nome ê sangue
E sangue dnha sodade ê

Message to Umbertona

Umbertona! Tomorrow
>I will set out for our island

What sign of love will you offer
>for me to take to your people

No! I am dry
>broken
>blindly scuttling like a crab

But have you
>No exiles' ballad

From those with neither
>morning nor dusk
>for me to bring to the voice of our people?

Go! Tell Sao Vicente
That my body's shadow is a cross
Far from the sun of my home
>running to Africa
>running to Europe
>running to America
>running across the map
>running across the globe

Go! Tell Porto-Grande
Not to call me saudade

Because my name is blood
And the blood of this saudade is

C'ma sol dnha terra longe
Palmanhã
    Sperança na Monte Verde

Dnote
    dsupère na Monte Cara

Bai! bô dzê Monte Cara
C'ma sour dnha coraçon ê mar
E arve dnha corpe ê navi
C'se mar na costa
C'se pé na tchon
    n'orela d'munde ta bai
C'mo rio Jordão ta corrê
    p'iternidade de Criste

Recode! bai bô dzê
    pove de Tchuba Tchobê
C'ma se pedra di tchon ê letra
Planta dnh pê ê scola
        Paquê
Nha pé ê lorg
    nha pé ê grande
E munde
    ê um didal na nha dedona

Like the sun of the far land
Monte Verde
    the hope of the morning

Monte Cara
    night's despair

Go! Tell Monte Cara
That the sea is the sweat of my heart
That the sea is a ship and the tree of my body
Carries the sea on its back
Going on
    Barefoot to the world's edge
As the River Jordan runs
    To Christ's eternity

Message! Go and tell
    The people of Tchuba Tchobe
That if the stones on the earth are letters
The soles of my feet are a school
        Because
My feet are broad
    My feet are big
And the world
    is a thimble on one of my toes

Terra a terra

Que a terra é carne!
               agora e sempre
Já a criança nos falava dela
               Devorando-a
Não
   a terra das cicatrizes
Mas
   a terra que cicatriza
               E nem sempre
A poeira Que o sangue irriiga
Ou terra tecida
               na rosa-dos-ventos
Mas a terra!
       o polme da terra
               que o sangue bebe
E a criança diz
       «na ferida: saliva e terra vermelha»
E jamais
     a terra trazida
         polida
         no espelho da gáspea
Mas o bolor da terra
               que tal umbigo devora

Earth to Earth

That the earth is flesh
               Flesh now and always
Already the child was telling us so
               Devouring it
Not
   the scarred earth
But
   The earth that scars
That dust that blood will irrigate
Or the earth that is woven
               in the four winds' compass rose
But the earth!
      the earth as liquid
                     that the blood will drink in turn
And the child says
      in the wound there is spit and red earth
Never
      The earth brought
             to a fine polish
              in the mirror of a patent-leather shoe
But the earth as mould
              that this navel will devour

Porta de sol

I

Das Colinas de colmo
               com portas de sol
Descem crianças
               nuas e magras
                      como violas
As costelas dentro da cordas
Todas
   primogénitas
               do mesmo ventre
E filhas
      Do mesmo vulcão E da mesma viola
         Da mesma rocha E do mesmo grito

II

A ilha roda no rosto da criança
com a «vareta presa» na roda do vento

III

Nem sempre
A criança respira
               um pulmão
                       roto de mapas

E assim
      como as ilhas

Gate of the Sun

I

From the straw hills
    whose gates are the sun
Children descend
    naked and thin
      like guitars
ribs showing under the strings
All of them
  the first-born
    of the one belly
And daughters
  of the same volcano And of the same guitar
  Of the same rock and the same cry

II

The island revolves in the face of its child
There's a stick jammed in the wheel of the wind

III

The child does not
Always breathe
    its lung was
      torn from the map

And thus
  like the islands themselves

Ao pôr do Sol
Se alimentam
           de fonemas
Cada criança
É ditongo de leite
           com sangue nas vogais

At sunset
They are fed
           on phonemes
Each child
Is a diphthong of milk
                with blood in its vowels

Há navio morto na cidadela

Há navios mortos na cidade velha

Uma criança atravessa a ilha entre tambores
O arbusto da mão cheio de terra
E coloca as sementes perto das violas

Duas crianças contornam a boca da ribeira
Com um canto de galo na veia cava
                           E acordam
Com o nó dos dedos
A proa dos rostos
De remos mortos no ocidente

Três crianças dobram
              os degraus da comarca E
Arrancam da carne
              As âncoras do achamento
              As naus da descoberta

There Is a Dead Ship at the Citadel

There are dead ships at the old city

A child crosses the island to the sound of drums
A bush offers a handful of earth
And spreads the seeds near the ten-string guitars

Two children skirt the river-mouth
At cock-crow in the vena cava
                             With their knuckles
They awaken
The prows of their faces
From dreams of dead oars in the west

The children wander
              the stairways of the neighbourhood
And draw from the flesh
            The anchors of discovery
            The caravels of exploration

Konde palmanhã manchê

Ó konde
Ó konde palmanhã manchê
Konde note ftcha ftchode
E palmanhã manchê
C'pê plantode na tchon
E terra na coraçon
Konde sangue rasgâ na corpe
Arve de broçe aberte
E smente gritâ na rotcha
Tambor de boca verde
E daquel som
Ma quel sangue soldode
Nascê boca
      boca centrode
      boca rasgode
Na roda de sol

Ó konde palmanhã manchê
Sem dsuspère pundrode
Na bandêra de porta
Sem lanterna cinidide
Na robe de burre
Pa naufroge de navi
Sem navi quebrode
Na boca de pove
E mar bem olte! brobe!
            dsusperode

When Morning Breaks

Oh when
Oh when the morning breaks
And the night becomes more night
When the morning breaks
With its feet on the ground
And the earth in its heart
When blood flows from the body
Like a tree with open arms
And the seed shouts from the rock
Like a green-mouthed drum
And from that sound
That warrior's blood
Mouths are born
    Centred mouths
    Torn mouths
In the wheel of the sun

Oh when the morning breaks
Without hanging its despair
On the flag of the door
Without lighting torches
On the donkeys' tails
To bring wrecks
Without shipwrecks
On the people's tongues
Then the desperate sea – very high –
                            Bravo!
Will come to break on Praia Grande
On its fat sinful arms

Ben quebrâ na Praia Grande
Sês broçe gorde de pecode
E mar bem
Na se luxe
E na se grandèza!
Se mostre
De mar erguide na pêto
Se mapa bronque

Desenhode n'alma
Bem bidê na colónia dnha boca
Tod' aquel negoce dnha sangue ultramarine

Ó konde palmanhã manchê
E Criste bem dsê morada
El bem ta bem
Pa broçe direita de Monte Cara
C'se cobe d'enxada
Ma se calçon drill
C'se pê na tchon
Ma se dede quebrode
Bem sentâ
Na pedra radonde dnôs fogon
Sem tchuva na mon
Sem fraqueza na sangue
E sem corve na coraçon

Ó konde
Ó konde palmanhã manchê

And the sea will come
In its grandeur
Showing its mast
On the heart's rough seas
Its white map
Drawn on the soul

Will come to drink in my colonized tongue
All the history of my ultramarine blood

Oh when the morning breaks
And Christ descends from his dwelling
And comes
To the right arm of Monte Cara
With the handle of his hoe
And his drill shorts
Barefoot
With a split finger
And sits down
At our round cooking-stone
With no rain in his hand
No weakness in his blood
No crow in his heart

Oh when
Oh when the morning breaks

Ilha

Sol & semente: raiz & relâmpago
Tambor de som
                Que floresce
A cabeça calva de Deus

Island

Sun & seed: root and lightning-stroke
Drum of sound
              That flourishes
On the bald head of God.

Raiz & Rosto

De manhã! há rostos & ombros
        Que amadurecem árvores no horizonte
E o céu! na sua casca amarela
        Salpicada de formigas e estrelas
É um fruto indeciso que não tomba

        *

Rosto! do oásis do teu olho
Nem sempre o deserto cospe
Entre as rochas; um caroço lunar

                E

Dos seios da ilha ao corpo de África
O mar é ventre E umbigo maduro
E o arquipélago cresce
            Entre as ilhas Que se vestem
Entre mil ... milhão e uma
Mais outra árvore agora
Mais um arco-íris depois

        *

E o corvo desta horta te dirá!
        ó usufruto
Que do uso da ilha ao fruto dela
As mãos & pés do meeiro
        Já não pesam o céu

Root and Face

In the morning! there are faces and shoulders
        That ripen trees on the horizon
And the sky! in its yellow rind
        Sprinkled with ants and stars
Is fruit that hesitates to fall

*

Face! From your eye's oasis you can see
That the desert does not always spit
A fruit-stone like a moon between the rocks

                And

From the breasts of the island to the body of Africa
The sea is a belly And a ripe navel
And the archipelago grows
           Between the islands that adorn themselves
Between a thousand and a million plus one
One more tree now
One more rainbow afterwards

*

And the crow in this vegetable garden will tell you!
        oh the benefit
shared by the island with her offspring
The hands and feet of the tenant farmer

Na balança da terra
      Com abutres
      Menos abutres no teu sangue

               *

De manhã! há tambores & ombros
Que amadurecem rostos no horizonte

                        E

Se tu ilha! no teu cavalo de pedra
Estendes a goela e os membros
E respiras
      arboreamente a maresia
As salinas sangram
Pela dubla narina da alma
pela dubla narina que galopa

Um arbusto de só E um arvoredo de seduçãc...

É a raiz à procura do rosto
É a face à procura da seiva

               *

E ao meio-dia! o deserto
      no seu crânio de vida
Salpicado de sombre E de sol verde

   Already they no longer weigh the sky
On the scales of the earth
   With vultures
   Fewer vultures in your blood

    *

In the morning! there are drums and shoulders
That ripen faces on the horizon

         And

If you, island!, on your horse of stone
Open the throat, extend the limbs
And breathe
   As a tree breathes the sea air
The salt-beds bleed
Through the soul's twin nostrils
Through the twin nostrils at a gallop

A solitary bush is a grove of seduction . . .

And the root is in search of the face
And the face is in search of the sap

    *

And at noon! The desert
   in its living skull
Sprinkled with shade And the green sun

Já não fala à ilha
Já não fala à árvore
Do seu falo de solidão

Da solidão não só . . . mas solidária

No longer speaks to the island
No longer speaks to the tree
From its solitary phallus

Of solitude not loneliness but solidarity

Hoje queria ser apenas tambor no coração do imbondeiro

I

O sol era ainda
    moeda de pão
        sobre o poente

Quando
As buzinas do ódio
E as rodas do ódio
E o ódio dos homens
    com matrícula nos olhos
Atropelaram no ventre da mulher grávida
O mais novo dos filhos
        do povo de Cazenga

O poente era então
    moeda de sangue
        sobre a noite

Quando os homens
        que eram rostos e revólveres
Com bala nos olhos
Que eram espingardas e balas
        com pólvora nas veias
Ergueram
Sobre o ventre pacífico do povo de Cazenga

Today I Want Only to be a Drum in the Heart of the Baobab

I

The sun was still simply
        a coin of bread
                above the sunset

When
The sirens of hatred
And the wheels of hatred
And the hatred of men
        with the gaze of the conscripted
Ran over the youngest child
Of the people of Cazenga
                Still in his mother's womb

Then the setting sun became
        a coin of blood
                over the falling night
When the men
        Whose faces were like guns
Who gazed like bullets
        And whose veins were charged with powder
Erected
Over the peaceful womb of the people of Cazenga
A rainbow
        of pain

Um arco-íris

        de dor
        de pânico
        de vísceras
        de sangue

II

E enquanto a noite
        debruçada sobre a noite
Bebia da boca
        das balas assassinas
O alto sangue
        do povo de Cazenga

As Forças d'Europa
        ressonavam
Com lâmpadas E vitrais nos olhos
E um cravo vermelho
        entalado na garganta

Não cubram! Irmãos
O rosto do povo de Cazenga
Com o escudo vermelho do ódio
Com o verde escudo da angústia

É dá árvore do Amor
        que se constrói

    panic
    viscera
    blood

II

And while the night
    Crouched over the night
Drank from the mouth
    of the murdering guns
the noble blood
    of the people of Cazenga

European powers
    Resound
In their eyes there are candles and stained glass windows
There are red carnations
    wedged in their throats

Brothers! Don't hide
The face of the people of Cazenga
With hatred's red shield
And the green shield of grief

It is from the tree of Love
    We make
The coffin
And our canto of despair
    With which since yesterday

O caixão
E a canção do nosso desespero
        que desde ontem
Erguemos bem alto
O sangue do povo de Cazenga
A alvorada
        que rebenta
        no caração do Imbondeiro

We have ennobled
The blood of the people of Cazenga
The dawn
               that breaks
               in the baobab's heart

Pólen para a tua boca

I

Que a paz venha
        pelo pé & polén das árvores de Boé

Avivar
        na dupla boca da terra
        na boca dupla dos mortos
            Os tambores de tanta guerra

E nasça – Amílcar! uma pirâmide intacta
No lugar do rosto
Onde o deserto do teu voo repousa

II

Oh lençol amargo da África viva
Que o rosto de Conakry não seja
        o corpo E o espírito
        Do mesmo coágulo de sangue

E que as balas de Janeiro
E as valas de Novembro
        não misturem teu sangue – Amílcar
À mesma moeda de corrupção

III

Oh raiz traída no bolor da côdea

Pollen for Your Mouth

I

Let peace come
> on foot & in pollen from the trees of Boe

To reawaken
> in the double mouth of earth
> in the double mouth of the dead
>> The drums of so many wars

Let there be born – Amílcar! a perfect pyramid
To represent your face
Where you rest in your desert flight

II

O bitter winding-sheet of living Africa
That the face from Conakry should not be
> the body and the spirit
> Of the same clot of blood

And let January's bullets
And November's ditches
> not mingle your blood – Amílcar
With the same corrupt currency

III

O root betrayed by the mildewed crust
From sun to shade

De sol à sombra
Não há lâmina que resista à árvore
   De sílaba & sílabas

Que vão
  pelo tambor da terra
    Que o espírito soletra

E de cratera em cratera
 de savana em savana
    Emergem! Amílcar

Colinas de mar alto
   primogénitas do teu sonho! onde
As flores de Septembro
     alçam
  no tronco do mesmo drama
O povo E a glória
  Da tua concha bivalve

There is no lamina that can resist the tree
>	of syllable and syllables

Let them go
>	through the drum of the earth
>>		Let the spirit spell it out

And from volcano to volcano
>	From savannah to savannah
>>		Rise again! Amílcar

The high seas' hills
>	where your dream was born! Where
The flowers of September
>>		raise up
>	on the trunk of this permanent story
The people And the glory
>	Of your double-mouthed conch

Mestiço: mestiça

Sol & carvão que une
O corpo e a alma da labareda
      ou
Febre que canta no acro-íris
            da carne Que sangra
A guerra & paz de todos os sonhos

Pilão & mó de pedra
Que rompe o caos da secura dos séculos
      ou
Parábola do amor que dança
Entre o verbo E o apocalipse

Árvore & tambor numa viola madura
      ou
Violão & viola que une
As mãos e os pés que gotejam
Pelo arquipélago dos dedos
      o trovão & relâmpago de Santa Bárbara

Mestizo : Mestiza

Sun and carbon joining
The body and soul of the flame
      or
Fever singing in the rainbow
                    flesh That bleeds
Its war & peace in dreams

Mortar and millstone
That wear the dry centuries down
      or
Parable of love that hovers
Between logos and apocalypse

Tree and drum of the ancient viola
      or
Guitar and viola that joins
The hands and feet that dance
Across the fingers' archipelago
      in Santa Barbara's thunderclap and lightning

Oráculo

Quando o arquipélago aperta
                     perto! longe
          A mão dos continentes

Quando a ilha rasga no deserto
              uma cicatriz de pedra
Jamais o crânio de sol! no mastro da solidão . . .
Uma pedra no deserto + um dragoeiro
Um anjo da guarda! no útero da paisagem

         Não! na ilha

Toda palavra é útero de sete pedras
         E
Toda a pedra é um poeta bizzexto
Leva quatro anos de pudor
E quarenta & tantos de paixão
Para inundar o deserto da estiagem
Com o dilúvio de chama que bebe
Nas crateras do jazz & batuque da esperança

Oracle

When the archipelago squeezes
                       The hand of the continents
        now near, now far

When the island carves in the desert
        a scar of stone
Never the skull of the sun! On the mast of solitude . . .
In the desert a stone + a dragon-tree
A guardian angel! in the womb of the landscape

        No! On the island

Every word is the womb of seven stones
        And
Every stone is a poet born in a leap year
It takes four years' humility
And forty-odd's passion
To inundate the desert
With the tide of flame that drinks
From the craters of jazz and drumming

A cesariana dos três continentes

Antes
      da moeda do corpo Ao capital da alma
Antes da luz
      no mar da memória
E da pedra & vento na erosão do rosto
Éramos no verão da terra
          A semente sem primavera
Éramos a exclamação
              Do lon na lonjura
Dando
      Pernas aos montes E braços às montanhas
Dando face & sentido
      Às dunas do mar alto
Que respiram
         as coxas
         os seios
         o sexo de Sahel

Lembro-me de ti! na África do teu ventre
Interrogando-se
         sobre o istmo + a
         proa do nosso destino
Quando pólos e penínsulas de maremoto
Rasgaram & rasgavam
No vórtice da vida! na fractura da terra
          A cesariana dos três continentes

The Caesarean of Three Continents

Before
    the body was coin and the soul Kapital
Before the light
    on the remembered sea
And the erosion of the face by stone and wind
We lived inside the summer of the earth
        The seed that had no spring
We were the exclamation
          Of the 'di' in distance

We gave
    Legs to the hills and arms to the mountains
Gave a face and a meaning
    To the dunes of the high seas
That breathe out
        the thighs
        the breasts
        the sex of the Sahel

I remember you! In the Africa of your womb
Enquiring of yourself
        about the isthmus + the
        prow of our destiny
When poles, peninsulas and tidal waves
Tore and tore in the vortex of life! In the fracture of earth
        The Caesarean of the three continents

Ficamos umbigos de pedra
                               Em rodopio
Entre a pele e o osso das estações
Ficámos então ilha + ilha
                               sobre o vento
                 pelo arquipélago da evasão

Assim! foi a pronúncia
                 Antes & depois do 1.º dia + a
Erosão da crónica
                 na boca da <<Rotcha Scribida>>

We became navels of stone
                revolving
Between the skin and bone of the seasons
We became island and island
                beyond the wind
                    in the evasive archipelago

Thus it was pronounced
                Before & after the 1st day + the
Erosion of the chronicle
                In the mouth of the Written Stone

Passo pelos dias

Passo pelos dias
E deixo-os negros
Mais negros
Do que a noute brumosa.

Olho para as coisas
E torno-as velhas
Tão velhas
A cair de carunchos.

Só charcos imundos
Atestam no solo
As pegadas do meu pisar
E fica sempre rubro vermelho
Todo o rio por onde me lavo.

E não poder fugir
Não poder fugir nunca
A este destino
De dinamitar rochas
Dentro do peito . . .

I Pass Through the Days

I pass through the days
And leave their blackness
Blacker
Than the foggy night

I look at things
And age them
Till woodworm rots them
Only filthy swamps

Of all the earth attest
That here I left a footprint
And where I wash myself
The river runs blood-red

To be unable to escape
To be unable ever to escape
And meet that destiny
That dynamites the rockfall in the heart.

Girassol

Girassol
Rasga a tua indecisão
E liberta-te.

Vem colar
O teu destino
Ao suspiro
Deste hirto jasmim
Que foge ao vento
Como
Pensamento perdido.

Aderido
Aos teus flancos
Singram navios.

Navios sem mares
Sem rumos
De velas rotas.

Amanheceu!

Orça o teu leme
E entra em mim
Antes que o Sol
Te desoriente
Girassol!

Sunflower

Sunflower
Renounce your indecision
Free yourself

Come
Stake your destiny
On the breath
Of this stiff jasmine
That flees on the wind
Like a lost train of thought

There are ships
On either hand
Compelled to sail with you

Ships without seas
Without bearings, lost
Dismasted ships

Dawn has broken!

Steer to windward now
And enter me
Before the sun
Disorients you
Sunflower!

Afterword

Corsino Fortes's work invites us to explore connections that transcend individual experience, illustrating how language bridges our multifaceted identities and communities. In 'Message to Umbertona', he asks us: *What sign of love will you offer / for me to take to your people?*

Daniel Hahn and Sean O'Brien's smooth translations of this collection prompt us to reflect on significant themes such as cultural and ancestral identity, the blending of heritages, and the correlation between landscapes, the body and the spirit. In the same poem, the speaker asserts *the sea is the sweat of my heart / …the sea is a ship and the tree of my body.*

This passage directly connects the body with the landscape – specifically, the sea and the tree. The way the sea is described suggests that the speaker's emotional or spiritual essence is linked with the physical landscape.

Similarly, French philosopher Gaston Bachelard writes that our homes and surroundings reflect our inner selves, highlighting that who we are is shaped by both our experiences and our environments.

We are also drawn to consider the movement and power of memory through lines such as *the blood of this suudade is / Like the sun of the far land.* These evoke a deep sense of loss and longing where the speaker seems to call on the memory of home and the people left behind.

Another poem that subtly engages with memory is 'Proposition': *Year by year / skull by skull / Faces circle / the eye of the island.* Here, the repetition of *year by year* and *skull by skull* suggests the passage of time, the cyclical nature of memory, and how the past continues to circle and influence the present.

In 'Pollen for your Mouth', we are reminded that memories, like the rhythm of the drum, move through generations, linking the living to the ancestors and giving voice to history's struggle: *Let them go / through the drum of the earth / Let the spirit spell it out.*

Fortes's mesmerising work has reminded me that our personhood extends beyond our family and biology. As in 'When Morning Breaks': *blood flows from the body / Like a tree with open arms.*

In my journey as a poet, I've often felt the pull of my cultural roots intertwined with the challenges of living in a second language, which has led me to appreciate the complex relationship between language and meaning and how they can build and strengthen ties across cultural divides. This tension is reflected in 'There Is a Dead Ship at the Citadel': *A child crosses the island to the sound of drums / A bush offers a handful of earth / And spreads the seeds near the ten-string guitars.*

The poem's imagery explores the connection between language, memory, and cultural identity. To me, the dead ships symbolise past struggles, while the child's journey, guided by the rhythm of drums, represents the passage of history and the continuous quest for understanding. Through this imagery, the poem reflects the way language bears the weight of history and influences our sense of self across different cultures.

I grew up in the Philippines, not surrounded by books, but with rich oral history in my grandfather's folktales and songs. In England, my mother's linguistic mishaps, as well as my own, gave me an appreciation for the literal and metaphorical power of language. These experiences taught me that growth emerges from change and the beauty and influences that envelop us underscore our interconnected journeys. Just like in Fortes's fluid form, free and unbound. He states: *the archipelago grows / Between the islands that adorn themselves.*

Just as each island in an archipelago holds its unique narrative, we also carry distinct stories shaped by our experiences, reinforcing our bonds. How we relate to others and the signs of love we offer each other strengthen the ties that bind.

Fortes warns, *Not to call me saudade / Because my name is blood*. His assertion that he is more than a term for longing or nostalgia highlights the complexity of diasporic identity. We are more than the culmination of our longings. We carry blood, ancestry, and endurance.

The idea that *the soles of my feet are a school* resonates deeply with me. My journey as a healer and caregiver (as a migrant teenager, a British nurse, and now as a new mother) has been enriching. I've learned important lessons from every community I encountered at every stage of my life. Fortes's metaphor reminds us that our journeys are connected; they exist for lessons. As he puts it: *the world / is a thimble on one of my toes*. Every step we take adds to our shared understanding and growth. Nature's resilience, wisdom, and power remains present, for it is not only *the scarred earth / But / The earth that scars*.

In my work as a nurse, I see how each patient's physical and emotional story reflects natural struggles. Just as my patients face chronic and acute conditions and uncertainty, the earth deals with droughts, wildfires and climate change. Both show a deep resilience and the ability to heal despite challenges. Fortes's work highlights the many ways humans, nature and power are threaded together. Our relationship with the planet reminds us that it is also a sacred part of our journey and who we are.

There is deep healing in both language and nature. While we inherit much through blood – illness, trauma, history – what gets passed down can also change. Just as *blood flows from the body / Like a tree with open arms*, this idea of transformation is essential. It powerfully emphasises our capacity to adapt and grow. There is agency and urgency in our shared suffering and longing. The poems urge us to embrace life beyond words as *the seed shouts from the rock*.

I am captivated by Fortes's vision of life's essence, which

emphasises the importance of experiencing and enduring pain. As a nurse, I understand that healing often involves suffering: a fractured bone causes inflammation, an open wound results in bleeding, and we perceive the world in shades of grey before its colours return and restoration occurs.

Healing is painful, yet with the love of our communities and the inspiration of our landscapes, we learn to move with pain in our roles as healers and artists. In Fortes's words, even a child understands that *in the wound there is spit and red earth*. Language, most importantly, is a force of resilience and renewal. It is capable of nurturing growth and healing. In Fortes's work, language is described as *the womb of seven stones*, highlighting its profound impact as both a birthright and a nurturing force. And in my journey as a new mother, though English is the primary language at home, I naturally utter Filipino words to my daughter, like Mahal kita (I love you) and Tama na (That's enough).

These phrases are more than just words. They connect my past, the people I care about, and the landscapes and communities that nurture me. I utter these words as talismans to my daughter. The imagery of *every stone is a poet* connects words with creation and individuality, just as the expressions I pass to my daughter carry not only meaning but ancestral legacy.

Fortes's skilful depiction of the strengths and vulnerabilities of both language and nature promotes the need for the creation of more lasting bonds and honours the legacy of our shared experiences.

I hope that readers will make their own connections when reading Fortes's poetry, just as I hope his poems will remind them that we are not just an island but an archipelago.

Romalyn Ante

Photo credit: Crispin Hughes

Corsino Fortes (1933-2015) was born in Mindelo on Cape Verde's São Vicente island. He worked as a teacher and a lawyer; he served as Cape Verde's ambassador to Portugal; and he was a judge in Angola. Fortes's first book, *Pão & Fonema* [Bread & Phoneme] appeared in 1974 and made an immediate impact. 1974 was a momentous year for Portugal and its African colonies as it was the year in which Portugal's dictator Salazar was overthrown, an act which began the process that led to the decolonisation of the Cape Verde Islands in 1975. After *Pão & Fonema* he published *Arvore e Tambor* [Tree and Drum] (Publicações Dom Quixote Lisbon) in 1986. He finished what he had long seen as a trilogy in 2001 with *Pedras de Sol & Substância* which was collected with the previous two books under the title *A Cabeça Calva de Deus* [The Bald Head of God] (Publicações Dom Quixote Lisbon).

Photo credit: John Lawrence   Photo credit: S. Chadawong

Daniel Hahn is a writer, editor and translator with about a hundred books to his name. He is currently co-editing a collection of Brazilian short stories, translating a Peruvian novel and writing a book about Shakespeare.

Sean O'Brien's eleventh collection, *Embark* appeared from Picador (2022). Recent publications include the chapbook *Impasse: for Jules Maigret* (Hercules editions, 2023), *Otherwise* (2023) and *Juniper* (2024), both from Dare-Gale. His work has received the T.S. Eliot and Forward prizes. His translations include the Inferno and the poems of Abai Kunanbayuli. He is Emeritus Professor of Creative Writing at Newcastle University.

Romalyn Ante is a Filipino-British writer born and bred in Lipa, Philippines. Her debut poetry collection, *Antemetic For Homesickness*, is published by Chatto & Windus, which was an Irish Times Best Poetry Book of 2020. Chatto also published her second collection *Agimat* in 2023. She is co-founding editor of *harana poetry*, a magazine for poets who write in English as a second or parallel language.

About the Poetry Translation Centre

Set up in 2004, the Poetry Translation Centre is the only UK organisation dedicated to translating, publishing and promoting contemporary poetry from Africa, Asia, the Middle East and Latin America. We introduce extraordinary poets from around the world to new audiences through books, online resources and bilingual events. We champion diversity and representation in the arts and forge enduring relations with diaspora communities in the UK. We explore the craft of translation through our long-running programme of workshops which are open to all.

The Poetry Translation Centre is based in London and is an Arts Council National Portfolio organisation. To find out more about us, including how you can support our work, please visit: www.poetrytranslation.org.

About the World Poet Series

The *World Poet Series* offers an introduction to some of the world's most exciting contemporary poets in an elegant pocket-sized format. The books are presented as dual-language editions, with the English and original-language text displayed side by side. They include specially commissioned translations and completing each book is an afterword essay by an English-language poet, responding to the translations.